DATE DUE

Chickens

by Peter Brady

Bridgestone Books
an Imprint of Capstone Press

Bridgestone Books are published by Capstone Press
818 North Willow Street, Mankato, Minnesota 56001
Copyright © 1996 by Capstone Press

Library of Congress Cataloging-in-Publication Data
Brady, Peter. 1944–
    Chickens/Peter Brady
    p. cm.
    Includes bibliographical references and index.
    Summary: Introduces the most common bird in the world by presenting facts about its
    physical characteristics, what it eats, where it lives, and the eggs which it lays.
    ISBN 1-56065-347-7
    1. Chickens--Juvenile literature. [1. Chickens.] I. Title.
SF487.5.B735 1996
636.5--dc20

                                                        95-54167
                                                          CIP
                                                           AC

Photo credit
All photos by William Muñoz. William is a freelance photographer. He has a
B.A. from the University of Montana. He has taken photographs for many
children's books. William and his wife live on a farm near St. Ignatius,
Montana, where they raise cattle and horses.

Table of Contents

Words in **boldface** type in the text are defined in the Words to Know section in the back of this book.

What Is a Chicken?

The chicken is the most common bird in the world. People raise chickens mostly on farms. Chickens are raised to lay eggs or to be eaten.

Roosters and Hens

Male chickens are called roosters. A rooster has a red **comb** on top of his head and **wattles** hanging from his face. Female chickens are called hens. They lay eggs and teach the young chicks how to live.

What Chickens Look Like

Chickens have plump bodies, silky feathers, and two strong feet. They have wings but cannot fly very far. Chickens can be striped, spotted, or solid colors. Hens weigh from two to 14 pounds (one to six kilograms). Roosters sometimes weigh more.

Where Chickens Live

Chickens live in a henhouse or chicken **coop,** often with a yard outside. Some families keep chickens in their backyard. Chickens like to be in the chicken yard so they can scratch for food.

What Chickens Eat

Chickens are fed grains and chicken feed. They scratch the ground for seeds, insects, and grass. Chickens can eat table scraps such as potatoes and bread, too.

Different Kinds of Chickens

There are more than 50 different **breeds** of chickens. Some of them are Rhode Island Red, Leghorn, Cornish, Ancona, and Wyandotte. Some breeds are raised just for show.

Eggs

One hen lays from 60 to 150 eggs a year. The eggs can be white, brown, or speckled. If the eggs are not **fertilized**, they can be used for eating.

Chicks

If eggs are fertilized, they can become chicks. Hens must sit on the fertilized eggs for three weeks to keep them warm. When the chicks are ready, they break out of their shells.

What Chickens Give Us

Chickens give us the eggs we buy in the store. Almost all chickens end up as meat for eating. Chicken is one of the most popular foods in the world.

Literary Connection: A Fable from Aesop

The Milkmaid and Her Pail

A woman was going to market with a pail of milk balanced on her head. She started planning.

With the money from the milk, she would buy a dozen eggs. The eggs would hatch, and she would sell the chickens and buy a beautiful dress. The dress would make everyone jealous, but she would just stick her nose in the air.

As she thought this, she stuck her nose in the air and the pail fell off her head. All her plans were now just a puddle on the ground.

The moral of the story is do not count your chickens before they hatch.

Words to Know

breed—group of animals that come from the same ancestors

coop—small cage or building for chickens

comb—red, crownlike growth on top of a chicken's head

fertilized—the condition of an egg after a rooster and hen come together to produce a chick

wattles—loose flaps of skin hanging from both sides of a rooster's face

Read More

Burton, Robert. *Egg.* New York: Dorling Kindersley, 1994.

Fowler, Allan. *The Chicken or the Egg?* Chicago: Children's Press, 1993.

Hariton, Anca. *Egg Story.* New York: Dutton Children's Books, 1992.

Wallace, Karen. *My Hen is Dancing.* Cambridge, Mass: Candlewick Press, 1994.

Index